D1266052

Weapons of the Vikings /

4/09

J355.82
W

BLAZERS

WEAPONS OF WAR

WEAPONS OF THE

VIKINGS

by Matt Doeden

Reading Consultant:
Barbara J. Fox
Reading Specialist
North Carolina State University

Content Consultant:
Professor Terje I. Leiren
Scandinavian Studies
University of Washington, Seattle

Capstone
press

Mankato, Minnesota

Blazers is published by Capstone Press,
151 Good Counsel Drive, P.O. Box 669, Mankato, Minnesota 56002.
www.capstonepress.com

Library of Congress Cataloging-in-Publication Data
Doeden, Matt.
      Weapons of the Vikings / by Matt Doeden.
      p. cm. — (Blazers. Weapons of war)
      Includes bibliographical references and index.
      Summary: "Describes the weapons of Viking warriors, including
hand-to-hand combat weapons, long range weapons, defenses, and
transportation" — Provided by publisher.
      ISBN-13: 978-1-4296-2335-3 (hardcover)
      ISBN-10: 1-4296-2335-7 (hardcover)
      1. Vikings — Warfare — Juvenile literature. 2. Weapons — Scandinavia —
History — Juvenile literature. I. Title.
DL66.D64 2009
623.4089'3950902 — dc22   2008030853

Editorial Credits
Mandy Robbins, editor; Alison Thiele, set designer; Kyle Grenz, book designer;
      Jo Miller, photo researcher

Photo Credits
Alamy/Arco Images/R. Hicker, 29 (leather helmet); Arctic Images/
      Ragner Th Sigurdsson, 28, 29 (shield); Classic Image, 13;
      Ladi Kirn, 16–17; North Wind Picture Archives, 22; Rob Walls,
      19 (axes); Simon Pentelow, 19 (bows and arrows); Steve Sant,
      10–11 (sax in sheath)
Art Resource, N.Y./British Museum, 8–9 (sword), 18 (sword); HIP, 4–5;
      Werner Forman, 14
Corbis/Bettmann, 6
Getty Images Inc./Jeff J. Mitchell, cover (ax); National Geographic/
      Michael Hampshire, 27; The Bridgeman Art Library/
      Viking, 18 (spearhead)
Granger Collection, New York, 23
hurstwic.org, 10–11 (sax and sheath), 18 (sax), 19 (halberds); iStockphoto/Jaroslaw Baczewski, 26; Lief Norman, cover (helmet);
      Manuel Velasco, 25, 29 (chainmail); Nicolette Nelsh,
      cover (armor), 29 (armor)
Mary Evans Picture Library, 15, 21; Douglas McCarthy, 9

TABLE OF CONTENTS

FIERCE WARRIORS

Swords flashed in the sunlight. Viking raiders rushed through a village. They grabbed valuables and burned buildings.

raider — someone who makes a sudden, surprise attack on people

Vikings were warriors and explorers from northern Europe. They raided European villages between the years of 700 and 1100. Their fierce weapons helped them take whatever they wanted.

WEAPON FACT

The Vikings sailed to North America almost 500 years before Christopher Columbus.

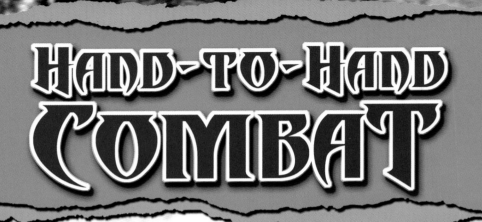

HAND-TO-HAND COMBAT

Only the richest Vikings had swords. They were the most expensive and prized Viking weapons. Their double-edged blades hacked through enemy armor.

WEAPON FACT

Many Viking warriors named their swords.

iron Viking sword

A sax was a cutting tool that doubled as a sword. It was a long knife with a single-edged blade. A curved sax was called a scramasax.

sax in sheath

sax

sheath

Spears were the most common Viking weapons. They had long wooden shafts and iron heads. Warriors thrust heavy spears into enemies. They threw lighter ones.

shaft — the long, narrow rod of a spear

head — the blade at the top end of a spear

WEAPON FACT

Skilled warriors could throw two spears at once.

spear

13

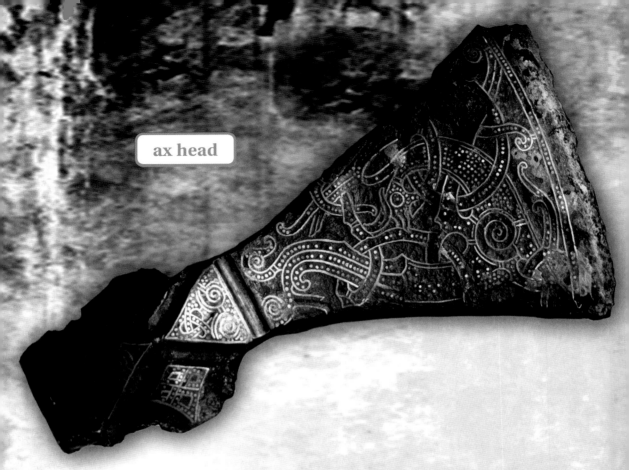

ax head

Battle-axes sliced through enemies
with amazing force. A Viking battle-ax
had an iron blade on a wooden handle.
Some battle-axes were small. Others were
as tall as a man.

battle-ax

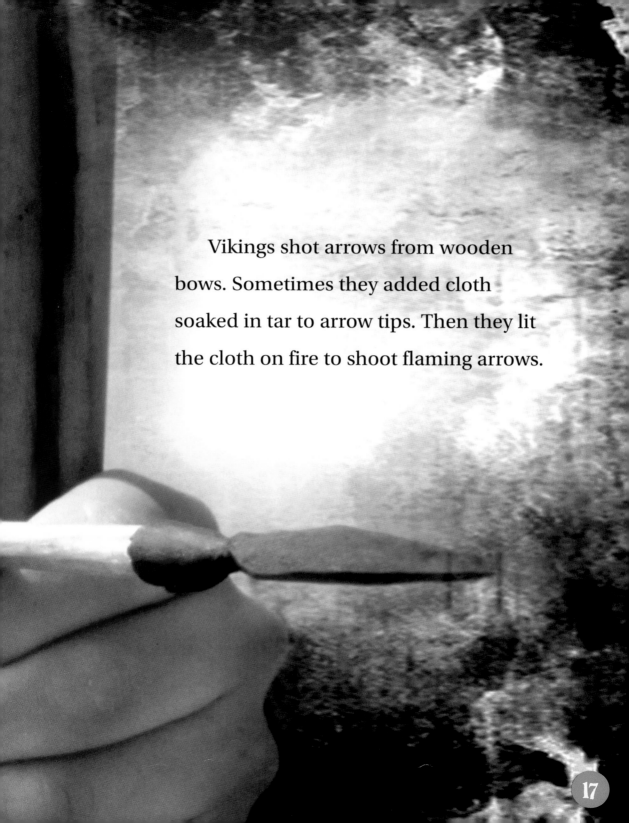

Vikings shot arrows from wooden bows. Sometimes they added cloth soaked in tar to arrow tips. Then they lit the cloth on fire to shoot flaming arrows.

HANDHELD WEAPONS

sword

spearhead

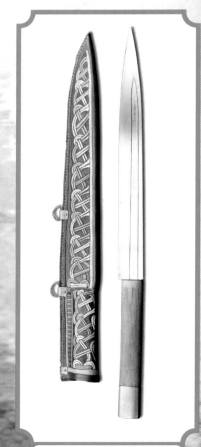

sax and sheath

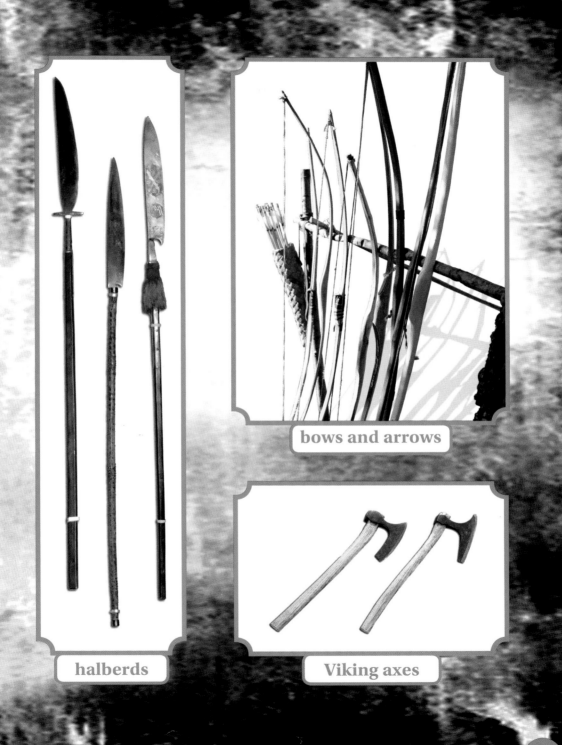

halberds

bows and arrows

Viking axes

LEGENDARY LONGSHIPS

Viking longships could be powered by sails or rowers. A longship was sturdy enough for the open sea. But it was small enough to travel along coasts or in rivers.

WEAPON FACT

Vikings sometimes carved the heads of beasts onto the fronts of their ships.

A longship could carry 50 warriors
or more. Dozens of ships would travel
together. These fast ships could sneak
up on a village. Then warriors ran
ashore to raid the village.

WEAPON FACT

Viking enemies called longships
"dragon ships."

VIKING PROTECTION

A Viking warrior counted
on strong armor to protect him.
Rich warriors wore expensive
chain mail shirts. Others wore
armor made of leather.

chain mail — a type of armor made of woven
metal chains

leather armor

chain mail

WEAPON FACT

Armor made of reindeer skin was
sometimes stronger than chain mail.

25

iron helmets

Vikings wore helmets made of iron or leather. Helmets were shaped like simple caps. Some helmets had nose guards, but none had horns. That is a common **myth**.

myth — a false idea that many people believe

Round wooden shields protected Vikings in battle. A round piece of iron was placed in the center of each shield. The iron protected a warrior's hand.

Viking grave site

A warrior's weapons were important to him. Many warriors were buried with their weapons. Scientists have learned a lot about the Vikings by studying their graves.

DURABLE DEFENSES

chain mail

leather helmet

shield

leather armor

GLOSSARY

armor (AR-muhr) — a protective covering worn by warriors during battle

chain mail (CHAYN MAYL) — armor made from woven links of chain

head (HED) — the top end of a spear or ax, where the blade is

longship (LONG-ship) — a long, narrow ship with many oars and a sail

myth (MITH) — a false idea that many people believe

raider (RAYD-ur) — someone who makes a sudden, surprise attack on a place

sax (SAKS) — a short, straight, single-edged blade that could be used as a tool or a weapon

scramasax (SKRAM-uh-saks) — a short, single-edged blade with a curved handle that could be used as a tool or a weapon

shaft (SHAFT) — the long, narrow rod of a spear or an arrow

READ MORE

Binns, Tristan Boyer. *The Vikings.* Ancient Civilizations. Minneapolis: Compass Point Books, 2006.

Charman, Andrew. *Life and Times in the Viking World.* Life and Times. London: Kingfisher, 2007.

Doeden, Matt. *Weapons of the Middle Ages.* Weapons of War. Mankato, Minn.: Capstone Press, 2009.

INTERNET SITES

FactHound offers a safe, fun way to find educator-approved Internet sites related to this book.

Here's what you do:

1. Visit www.*facthound.com*
2. Choose your grade level.
3. Begin your search.

This book's ID number is 9781429623353.

FactHound will fetch the best sites for you!

INDEX